W9-AOI-698

Ages 4&5
Undercover
Heroes
OF THE BIBLE

Rainbow Publishers

Rainbow Publishers · P.O. Box 261129 · San Diego, CA 92196

Ages 4 & 5
Undercover Heroes of the Bible

Angela Bowen Herrmann
Donna Bowen McKinney

Dedicated to Jennifer and Jonathan, siblings and friends.
Thanks for a childhood rich with memories and love.

UNDERCOVER HEROES OF THE BIBLE/AGES 4&5
©2002 by Rainbow Publishers, second printing
ISBN 1-58411-010-4
Rainbow reorder# RB38072

Rainbow Publishers
P.O. Box 261129
San Diego, CA 92196

Illustrator: Chuck Galey
Editor: Christy Allen

Scriptures are from the *Holy Bible: New International Version* (North American Edition), ©1973, 1978, 1984 by the International Bible Society. Used by permission of Zondervan Bible Publishers.

Printed in the United States of America

Table of Contents

Memory Verse Index

Introduction

The familiar Bible stories with their familiar heroes are wonderful. We can learn a lot by telling these stories over and over again. But what about the less familiar people of the Bible? Most of us can remember parts of the stories of Moses, Noah or John the Baptist. However, the Bible is full of people who are not quite so famous or familiar to us. These "unsung heroes" were still an exciting part of God's story. There is much to be learned from studying about them, too.

These lessons are designed to be easy to use. There is a Bible story about each hero. Then there is a craft or activity to accompany each story. There are also word puzzles and mazes for many of the stories. These can be used as an activity for "early arrivals" during the class time, or as a take-home activity. The "Note to Families" on page 11 will help you collect supplies for the activities.

All of the crafts, activities, word puzzles and mazes in *Undercover Bible Heroes* were designed especially for four- and five-year-olds. The lessons are arranged in alphabetical order, but you can use them in any order you want. Once you select a lesson, the book guides you through the teaching and activity time.

Help your children learn to love these *Undercover Heroes* just as they love the familiar characters of the Bible.

Note to Families of Four- and Five-Year-Olds

We will be teaching exciting lessons about heroes of the Bible. You can help us learn by bringing the marked items below.

❑ adhesive bandages
❑ baking soda
❑ bird seed
❑ braid scraps
❑ buttons
❑ child-size brooms
❑ cookie dough
❑ corn starch
❑ cotton balls
❑ dish pans
❑ dish towels or cloths
❑ dishwashing gloves
❑ dishwashing liquid
❑ disposable hand wipes

❑ dry, round cereal
❑ dusting cloths
❑ empty baby food jars
❑ fabric scraps
❑ felt scraps
❑ foil pie plates
❑ gauze
❑ heart-shaped cookie cutters
❑ men's old shirts
❑ old newspapers
❑ paper towels
❑ peanut butter
❑ pine cones
❑ plastic spoons

❑ plastic sandwich bags
❑ ribbon scraps
❑ rick-rack
❑ rolling pins
❑ sand
❑ sandpaper
❑ small bean bag
❑ small paper sacks
❑ small, pocket-size mirrors
❑ small, scented candles
❑ spring-type clothespins
❑ towels
❑ wire coat hangers

Please bring in the items on _____.

Thank you for your assistance!

Note to Families of Four- and Five-Year-Olds

We will be teaching exciting lessons about heroes of the Bible. You can help us learn by bringing the marked items below.

❑ adhesive bandages
❑ baking soda
❑ bird seed
❑ braid scraps
❑ buttons
❑ child-size brooms
❑ cookie dough
❑ corn starch
❑ cotton balls
❑ dish pans
❑ dish towels or cloths
❑ dishwashing gloves
❑ dishwashing liquid
❑ disposable hand wipes

❑ dry, round cereal
❑ dusting cloths
❑ empty baby food jars
❑ fabric scraps
❑ felt scraps
❑ foil pie plates
❑ gauze
❑ heart-shaped cookie cutters
❑ men's old shirts
❑ old newspapers
❑ paper towels
❑ peanut butter
❑ pine cones
❑ plastic spoons

❑ plastic sandwich bags
❑ ribbon scraps
❑ rick-rack
❑ rolling pins
❑ sand
❑ sandpaper
❑ small bean bag
❑ small paper sacks
❑ small, pocket-size mirrors
❑ small, scented candles
❑ spring-type clothespins
❑ towels
❑ wire coat hangers

Please bring in the items on _____.

Thank you for your assistance!

Barnabas • A Good Steward

Sharing With Each Other

Acts 4:32-37 (read aloud)

Then tell the Bible story:

There was a special church in the city called Jerusalem. The people in the church loved God and they loved each other very much. The leaders in the church talked about Jesus. New people came to the church all the time.

The people in the church showed their love by sharing what they had with each other. If someone in the church needed food or clothes, then the other people in the church would help them buy the things they needed.

There was a man in this church named Barnabas. His name means "son of encouragement." Barnabas owned a piece of land. One day, Barnabas decided to sell the land. When he got the money from the person who bought the land, Barnabas brought the money to the church. Barnabas gave the money to the leaders in the church. He told them to use the money to help people who were in need.

Barnabas was like many other people in that church. They showed how much they loved each other by sharing with each other.

Talk It Over

1. What did the church in Jerusalem do when people needed help?
2. What did Barnabas do to show how much he loved God and the people in his church?
3. How can we show that we love people in our church?

Walking in God's Love

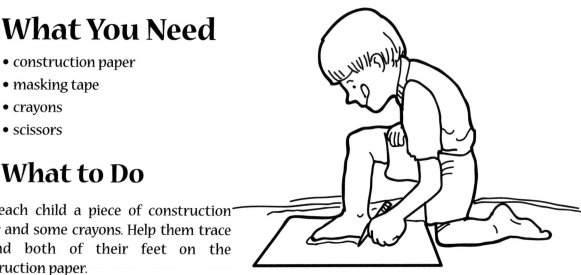

What You Need

- construction paper
- masking tape
- crayons
- scissors

What to Do

1. Give each child a piece of construction paper and some crayons. Help them trace around both of their feet on the construction paper.

2. Have the children draw or write in both of their feet tracings one thing they can do to show God's love to someone else. You might suggest things like visiting a shut-in, helping a new friend in class, playing a game with a younger brother/sister, etc.

3. After they finish drawing or writing on their "feet," help the children cut out the feet patterns. Then have the children help you tape all the feet patterns to the floor, making a path through the classroom.

4. Have the children line up. Lead them along the path, following the feet patterns. Stop and talk about the ideas for showing love that are described on each footprint.

Visit a shut-in.

Play a game with a friend.

Help a new friend.

Read to an elderly person.

Barnabas Fill-In

Barnabas looked for ways to help the other people in his church. One day he sold some of his land. Then he gave the money from the land to his church. The church used the money Barnabas gave to help people who were poor. You can be a helper in your church, too. How can you share with people who need help?

Write the missing words of the Bible verse on the blank lines below.

Do not _____
1

to do_____and to
2

_____ with
3

_____ . (Hebrews 13:16)
4

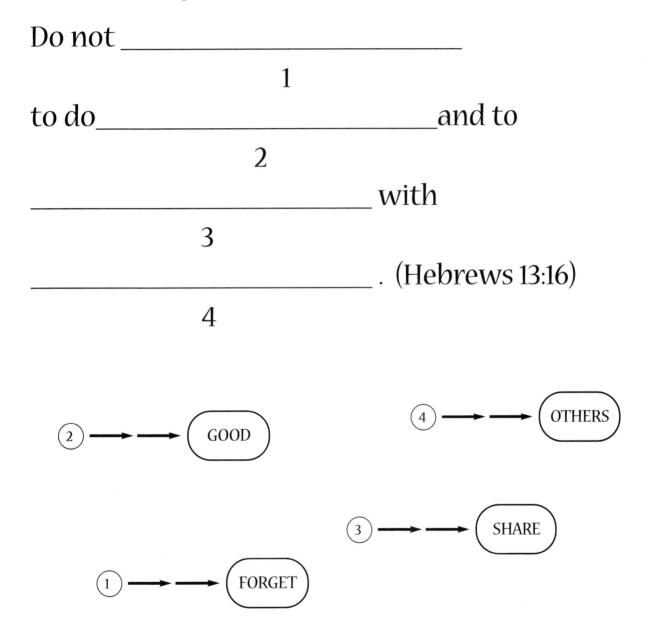

The answers are on page 96.

I Can Show Love

Barnabas understood how to share. He sold a piece of land that he owned and then he gave the money as an offering to the church. The money that Barnabas gave was used to help people who were in need. Read the statements below aloud and have the children take turns sharing an answer.

When my mother is busy fixing dinner, I can show love by:

When a girl moves to my town and comes to my class, I can show love by:

When my sister has lost her favorite book, I can show love by:

When my brother wants to play with my friends and me, I can show love by:

When my dad goes outside to work in the garden, I can show love by:

When my teacher asks for helpers to clean up the paint and brushes, I can show love by:

Do not forget to do good and to share with others.
Hebrews 13:16

The Blind Beggar • Praise for Healing

Memory Verse: Cast your cares on the Lord. (Psalm 55:22)

With Eyes that Can See

Luke 18:35-43 (read aloud)

Then tell the Bible story:

There was a man who was blind. Each day he sat by the side of the road and begged for money from people who walked down the road.

One day, Jesus came walking down the road. A crowd of people was following Jesus. The blind man heard the people coming. He wondered what was happening.

Someone told the blind man that it was Jesus who was coming. The blind man called out, "Jesus, Son of David, have mercy on me!" The people in the crowd told the blind man to be quiet. But still, he called out Jesus' name.

Jesus stopped and talked to the blind man. He asked the blind man, "What do you want Me to do for you?" The blind man told Jesus that he wanted to see. Right away, Jesus healed the blind man and he was able to see.

The man got up and followed Jesus. He praised God because now he could see! The other people in the crowd praised God, too. They were amazed and thankful.

Talk It Over

1. Why did the blind man call out to Jesus?
2. What did Jesus do for the blind man?
3. What did the blind man do after he could see?

Bird Feeder

What You Need

- pinecones
- yarn
- scissors
- peanut butter
- bird seed
- plastic spoons
- plastic sandwich bags
- bird pattern from page 19
- scissors
- tape

Before Class

Make a copy of the bird on page 19 for each child. Cut the yarn into 10" lengths, one per child. You will need one pinecone per child.

What to Do

1. Remind the children how Jesus cared about the blind man. Describe how God wants us to care for others and for His creation. Explain that the class will make bird feeders to help take care of the birds in your neighborhood.

2. Give each child a pinecone and a 10" length of yarn. Help the children tie the yarn to the top of the pinecone. You may want to wrap it around the cone a couple of times before you tie it to make sure that it is secure. Explain to the students that they will be able to use the yarn to attach the feeder to a tree branch.

3. Give each child a spoon and some peanut butter. Help the children slather peanut butter on the pinecone using the plastic spoon.

4. Help the children sprinkle bird seed onto the cone so that it sticks to the peanut butter.

5. Carefully stuff each pinecone inside a plastic sandwich bag so that the children can safely take them home.

6. Give each child a copy of the bird from page 19 to cut out and tape to the bag.

7. Instruct the students to ask an adult to help them fasten their bird feeder to a tree branch where they can watch the birds eat.

Cast your cares
on the Lord.

Psalm 55:22

Cast your cares
on the Lord.

Psalm 55:22

Eyes to See Game

What You Need

- bean bag
- crayons

What to Do

1. After you tell the story of Jesus healing the blind beggar, play this game.

2. Seat the children in a circle, either in chairs or on the floor.

3. Begin by saying, "Thank you, God, for eyes that see_____," and fill in the blank with one thing you can see in the classroom.

4. Toss the bean bag to a child. Have the child complete the same statement with something he or she sees in the room.

5. That child should then toss the bean bag to another child. Continue tossing the bean bag and naming things that can be seen until everyone has had a turn. If time allows, play the game again to give everyone a second turn.

6. Lead the children in a prayer, thanking God for giving us eyes that can see the beautiful world around us. Then read the instructions below and have the kids draw a picture in the box.

Calling Out to Jesus

The blind beggar could not see. So he called out to Jesus for help. Jesus stopped and talked to the blind man. The blind man told Jesus that he wanted to see. Jesus healed the man. Then the man got up and began praising God. All the people who were watching praised God, too. Everyone was happy that the blind man could see. Draw a picture in the box below of the blind man calling out to Jesus.

The Boy & a Lunch • A Sharer

Memory Verse: They all ate and were satisfied. (Mark 6:42)

The Loaves and Fishes

John 6:1-13 and Mark 6:30-44 (read aloud)

Then tell the Bible story:

Jesus was busy teaching people. A large crowd of more than 5,000 people were now following Jesus and the disciples. It was late in the afternoon. It would soon be time to eat dinner. But Jesus, the disciples, and all the people were far away from town. What would they eat?

The disciples looked for food, but all they could find was a boy with a small lunch. The lunch was just a few pieces of fish and some small loaves of bread. The boy gave Jesus his lunch.

Jesus told the disciples to have all the people sit down on the ground. Then Jesus thanked God for the food and presented the food to the disciples to give to the people. With just those two fish and five loaves of bread, Jesus fed a crowd of more than 5,000 people! Then after everyone had eaten, the disciples gathered up the leftovers. There were more than twelve baskets full of food!

At first, the lunch was just enough food for the boy. But when Jesus took the lunch, He created a miracle.

Talk It Over

1. What did the boy have for lunch?
2. What did Jesus do with the boy's lunch?

Fish and Loaves Rubbings

What You Need

- pattern of fish and loaves, page 23
- sandpaper
- paper
- crayons

Before Class

Make a copy of the fish and loaf patterns on page 23. Use the patterns to trace and cut out a fish and loaf from sandpaper for each child.

Jesus fed 5,000 people with just a boy's lunch.

What to Do

1. Give each child a sandpaper fish and loaf.

2. Show the children how to place a sheet of paper over each sandpaper pattern and use a crayon to rub over the paper so that the textured pattern of the fish or loaf shows on the paper. Have them make rubbings of several fish and loaves on the paper.

3. Write "Jesus fed 5,000 people with just a boy's lunch" at the top of each child's paper. Remind the children that Jesus used the boy's small lunch to perform a mighty miracle to feed so many people.

Sharing Maze

The boy shared his lunch with Jesus. You can share with the people you see each day, too. The boy in the picture below has to go to different places this week. Talk about how he can share with other people at each of these places.

My school

My home

My church

Playing with friends

They all ate and were satisfied.
Mark 6:42

The solution is
on page 96.

Feeding Picture

Draw a picture in the frame below of Jesus feeding the big crowd of people with the boy's lunch.

They all ate and were satisfied.
Mark 6:42

The Centurion • Full of Faith

summer 2003

Memory Verse: Stand firm in the faith. (1 Corinthians 16:13)

A Soldier With a Strong Faith

Matthew 8:5-13 (read aloud)

Then tell the Bible story:

One day Jesus was visiting a city called Capernaum. While He was there, a soldier came to Him and asked for help. The soldier told Jesus that a man at his house was very sick. The soldier was sad and worried because the man was so sick.

Jesus told the soldier that He would come to the house and make the man well. The soldier said that Jesus did not have to come to the house where the man was sick. Instead, the soldier believed that if Jesus just spoke the words then the man would be well. The soldier knew that Jesus did not have to visit the soldier's house and see the man who was sick to heal him.

Even Jesus was surprised that the soldier had such a great faith. The soldier believed that Jesus could heal the man with just the power in His words. Jesus said that He had not met anyone in the whole country who had showed faith like this soldier had. Right away Jesus told the soldier that the man was well. As soon as Jesus spoke the words, the man was well.

Talk It Over

talk, talk!

1. What does it mean to have faith? (believe in something, trust, etc.)
2. How did the soldier show that he had faith in Jesus?
3. Can we have faith today?

Standing Firm in the Faith

What You Need

- newsprint or poster paper (at least 6 feet long)
- washable tempera paint
- disposable pie plates
- paint brushes
- old newspapers
- paint smocks
- wet washcloths
- towels

STAND FIRM IN THE FAITH.
I CORINTHIANS 16:13

What to Do

1. Explain that the memory verse will be made into a mural for the classroom. Say the memory verse aloud.

2. Spread old newspapers on the floor to protect it. Then place the newsprint on top of the newspapers.

3. Help the children into paint smocks. Men's old shirts work well for smocks.

4. Write the memory verse in pencil on the newsprint so that it is centered on the paper. Pour some tempera paint in the pie plate and have the children take turns painting over the penciled letters of the Bible verse. Allow time for the paint to dry.

5. Have the children remove their socks and shoes and roll up their pant legs if they're wearing long pants. Help the children carefully dip the bottom of their feet in the paint. Then have them make footprints on the paper. Spread out the footprints so they circle the verse on the newsprint.

6. Be sure to wipe off and dry the children's feet before they put their socks and shoes back on.

7. After all the footprints are dry, display the mural in the classroom. Lead the children in saying the verse aloud.

Centurion Fill-In

A soldier (called a centurion) came to see Jesus. The soldier needed Jesus' help. A man at the soldier's house was very sick. The soldier asked Jesus to heal the man. The soldier believed that the man could be well if Jesus would just say the words for the man to be healed. Jesus spoke the words and right away, the man got well.

Jesus said that he had not met anyone

in the whole country who showed such a great

_____ .

To find the word that fills the blank, turn this page upside down.

The answer is on page 96.

Stand firm in the faith.
1 Corinthians 16:13

Centurion Word Balloons

The centurion, a soldier in the army, believed that Jesus could make his friend well. Jesus said that the centurion had great faith.

Write the words of the Bible verse in the correct order on the lines below. Talk about what it means to have faith.

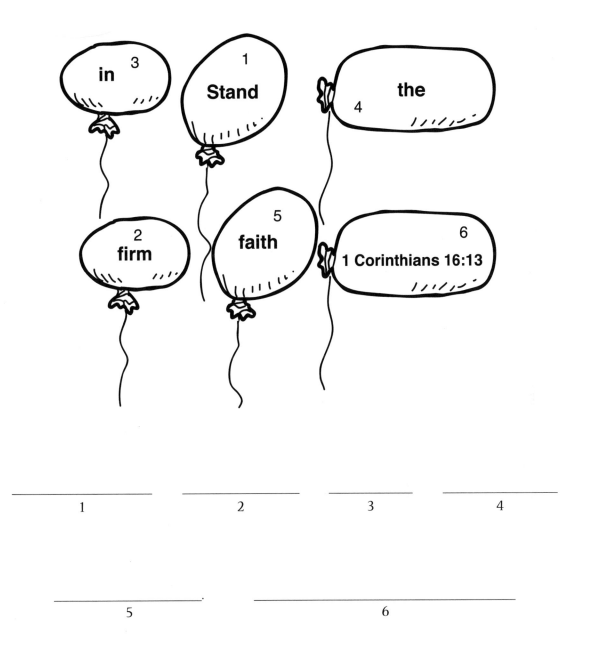

_____ _____ _____ _____
1 2 3 4

_____. _____
5 6

The answers are on page 96.

Deborah • A Wise Judge

Memory Verse: If any of you lacks wisdom, he should ask God…and it will be given to him.

(James 1:5)

Wisdom from God

Judges 4:4-9 (read aloud)

Then tell the Bible story:

When we read the Bible, we can learn about many people who followed and obeyed God. Deborah was a woman who obeyed God.

A long time before Jesus was born, Deborah was chosen to be the leader of the country of Israel. She was a wise leader who served God each day.

Deborah was also a judge for the people. When two people could not get along with each other, they would talk to Deborah. She would help the people solve their problems.

God gave Deborah wisdom to help other people with their problems. God wants each of us to be wise. If we ask God for wisdom, He will give it to us.

talk, talk! Talk It Over

1. What special jobs did Deborah have?
2. Deborah was famous for being a wise woman. How can we be wise like Deborah?

Judge Deborah Skit

What You Need

- Deborah cases below
- chair

Before Class

Make a copy of the Deborah cases below and cut them apart.

What to Do

1. Remind the children that Deborah was a leader for her people and that she obeyed God. Also remind them that people came to Deborah when they had problems or arguments and she helped them settle their disagreements.

2. Have one child sit in the chair to play the role of Deborah (if any of the boys are reluctant to play the part of Deborah, explain that there were other judges besides Deborah and that they were men).

3. Have the other children line up facing "Deborah." Let each child in line select one of the cases and read it aloud for them. Ask the child playing Deborah to tell how he or she would solve the problem.

4. As you work through the cases, let different children take turns playing the part of Deborah. Repeat some of the cases, if needed, giving different children a chance to respond as Deborah.

Deborah Cases

Tim and Steve both want to play with the blocks at the same time. What can they do?

Ashley is coloring and Erin wants to color, too. But Ashley won't share the crayons. What can they do?

The teacher has asked everyone to help pick up the toys in the room. But Tony and Megan are still busy working a puzzle. What can they do?

Maria's little brother is crying because he's unhappy. Maria's mom is busy trying to fix dinner for the family. What can Maria do?

Joey spilled the crayons but he didn't pick them up. Now the teacher is making everyone in the class pick up the crayons. What can Joey do?

Carlos is watching his favorite TV show. Carlos' mom asks him to help set the table for dinner. What can Carlos do?

Jason and Samantha both want to play with the jump rope at the same time. What can they do?

Sarah is watching a TV show. Her sister Bethany wants to watch a different TV show. What can they do?

Keisha and Billy always play together each day after school. They see that a new girl about their age has moved in a house down the street. What can they do?

Deborah's Memory Verse Code

Deborah loved and obeyed God. The people chose Deborah to be one of their leaders. Deborah had the job of helping people solve their problems when they could not get along with each other. Each day, people came to talk to Deborah. She listened and helped the people. Deborah was known for being a wise woman.

The Bible says that we can be wise people, too. We can become wise when we obey God and follow His plan for our lives. If we pray and ask God for wisdom, He is glad to give us wisdom, just like He did for Deborah.

Match the designs below. Write the words in the blanks to complete the memory verse. Then practice saying the verse aloud.

GOD   GIVEN   WISDOM   HIM   YOU

IF ANY OF _____ LACKS _____, HE SHOULD ASK _____

…AND IT WILL BE _____ TO _____.

— James 1:5

The answers are on page 96.

Elisha • A New Prophet

Memory Verse: We too will serve the Lord. (Joshua 24:18)

Called to Do a Special Job for God

1 Kings 19:15-21 (read aloud)

Then tell the Bible story:

Elijah the prophet was growing old. Elijah served God for many years. As a prophet, he preached God's message to the people and performed many miracles. But Elijah knew that it would soon be time for a new prophet to take his place. God told Elijah that the new prophet would be a man named Elisha. Elisha did not know that God had a special job for him to do. But he would soon find out because God was sending Elijah to tell him.

One day Elisha was out working in the fields. Elisha did not have a tractor like farmers do today. Instead, he had some oxen and a plow. Elisha plowed the field, getting it ready for seed.

While Elisha plowed, Elijah came to looking for him. Elijah took off his cloak (like a coat) and threw it around Elisha's shoulders. By doing this, Elijah showed that Elisha would be the next prophet for God.

Elisha knew that God was calling him to do a special job. Right away, he stopped plowing and left the oxen. Elisha told Elijah that he needed to say good-bye to his parents. Elisha hurried to say good-bye.

Elisha also burned his plow. This showed all the people that he would not be a farmer anymore. From then on, Elisha served God as a prophet. He left his family and friends and followed Elijah. Elijah taught Elisha what he knew about God. Then Elisha served God in a mighty way, just like Elijah had.

Talk It Over

1. Why did Elijah go looking for Elisha?
2. How did Elijah show that God was calling Elisha to do a special job?
3. How did Elisha answer God's call?
4. What are some jobs that you can do for God?

Finger Puppets

What You Need

- dishwashing gloves
- glue
- wiggle eyes
- yarn scraps
- fabric scraps
- scissors

Before Class

You will need one "finger" for each child. Cut the ends of the fingers off the gloves. The "fingers" will be used to make puppets.

What to Do

1. Ask the children to talk about what they want to be when they grow up (teacher, doctor, fireman, etc.) Explain that you will be making finger puppets to show the kinds of jobs they want to have when they grow up.

2. Give each child a glove "finger" and have them make the puppet by gluing on eyes, yarn for hair and fabric scraps for clothes.

3. Let the children use their finger puppets to act out what they want to be when they grow up. Have the rest of the class try to guess what the puppet is. Talk about how God can use us in our jobs to serve Him, like Elisha served God.

Elisha Memory Verse Scramble

Elijah the prophet had served God for many years. Now it was time for a new prophet. God chose Elisha to be the next prophet. Both Elijah and Elisha had special jobs — preaching God's Word to the people. The memory verse is scrambled up in the pictures below. Can you put the verse in the right order? When you do, write the verse in the spaces below.

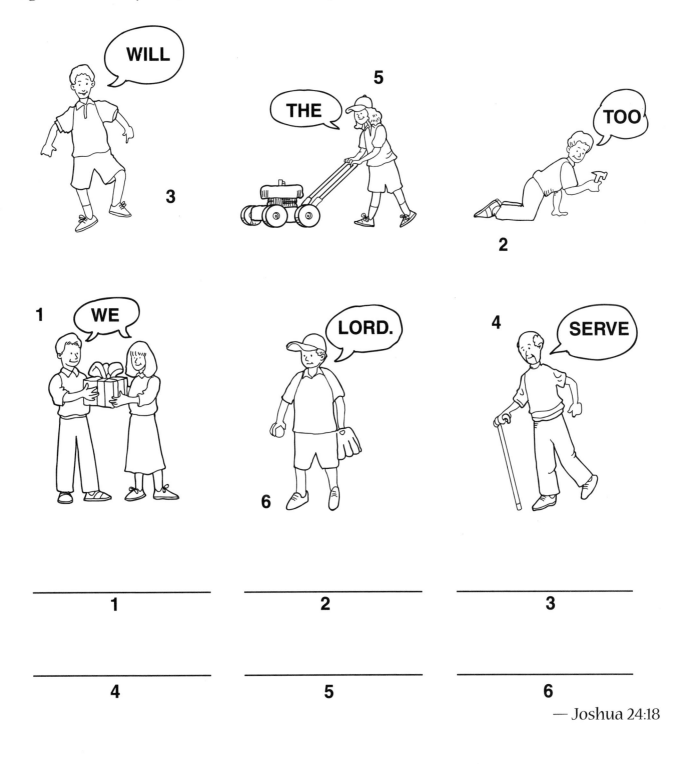

_____ _____ _____
    1   2   3

_____ _____ _____
    4   5   6

— Joshua 24:18

The answers are on page 96.

35

Epaphras • Believer in Prayer

A Man Who Prayed

Colossians 1:7, 4:12-13 (read aloud)

Then tell the Bible story:

Epaphras loved God very much. He was a busy worker for God. Epaphras helped to start a new church in a city called Colosse, where there had not been a church before.

After the church was started, Epaphras traveled to be with another preacher, named Paul, who was in Rome. Paul had been put in jail because some people did not want to hear him talk about God.

While Paul was in jail, Epaphras stayed with him to help him. Even though Epaphras was not living in Colosse, he still loved the people there very much. Prayer was one way that Epaphras showed his love for the people. The Bible says that Epaphras prayed very hard for the people in the church in Colosse. We can pray for anyone, at any time and anywhere.

Talk It Over

1. What did Epaphras do in the city of Colosse?
2. How did Epaphras show his love for the people in the church?

Love Cookies

What You Need

- prepared cookie dough
- oven
- red sprinkles
- heart-shaped cookie cutters
- rolling pin
- plastic sandwich bags
- yarn
- heart pattern from below
- pink or red construction paper
- scissors
- tape

Before Class

Duplicate the heart shape below on red construction paper for each child.

What to Do

1. Explain that the class will show love for their families by making Love Cookies.
2. Help the children roll out the cookie dough.
3. Give each child a turn at using the cookie cutters to cut out several cookies.
4. Have the children take turns spreading red sprinkles on their cookies.
5. Bake the cookies according to the package instructions.
6. While the cookies bake and cool, have the children make heart messages. To do this, help them cut a heart shape from construction paper and write a special message to their families on the heart ("I love you," "I love my family," "You are special to me," etc.).
7. After the cookies cool, have the children put the cookies in the sandwich bags. Tie a piece of yarn around the top of the bag to close it. Fasten the heart message to the bag with tape. Encourage the children to share the cookies with their families.

The Path to Rome

Epaphras loved God. He started a church in a city called Colosse. But then Epaphras needed to travel to a city called Rome to be with Paul, another preacher who was in jail because of his beliefs. Epaphras went to help Paul. Use your finger or a pencil to trace the road Epaphras must follow to get to Rome.

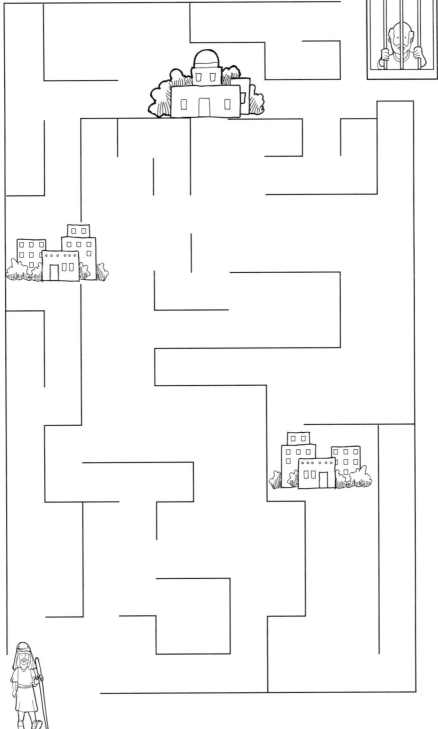

Pray for each other.
James 5:16

The solution is on page 96.

Showing Love

Epaphras loved the people in the church in Colosse. He showed his love by praying for the people all the time. How can you show love to your friends? Draw a picture in the box below of how you can show love to your friends.

Pray for each other.
James 5:16

The Loving Father • A Troubled Son

Memory Verse: God is love. (1 John 4:16)

Watching and Waiting

Luke 15:11-24 (read aloud)

Then tell the Bible story:

One day Jesus told this story to the people. There was a man who had two sons. The younger son decided that he was tired of living at home and working with his father. The son wanted to travel to far-away countries and spend his time having fun at parties. This made the father very sad. He didn't want to see his son leave home. But the son was grown up and he could leave home if he wanted. The son asked the father to give him some money to pay for his trip. The father gave his son the money.

The son traveled to far-away countries. When he got there, he spent his money on parties. Soon all of the money was gone. The only job that the son could find was feeding pigs. The son could not find any food, so he finally started eating the pigs' food.

Soon, the son knew that he should go home to his father. The son made a plan. He would go home and ask his father to forgive him for leaving home and spending all his money. Then the son would ask his father if he could work as a servant for him.

When the son got close enough to his home that he could see his house, guess who saw the son and came running out to meet him? His father! The father hugged and kissed his son. The father was happy that his son had come home! He called all the family together and they had a big dinner to celebrate the son's return.

Jesus told this story to help us see that God is like the father. Sometimes we do things wrong and get into trouble like the son. But God, our Father, still loves us and wants us to come back to Him.

Talk It Over

1. Why did the son leave home?
2. How did the father show that he loved his son?
3. How do we know that God loves us?

I Love My Family Mobile

What You Need

- wire coat hangers
- yarn or string
- scissors
- markers or crayons
- white poster board
- hole punch

Before Class

Cut the white poster board into rectangles about 3" x 4" in size. Have enough rectangles so the children can draw each of their family members on a piece. Cut the string or yarn into pieces about 6" to 8" long. You will need one hanger per child.

What to Do

1. Remind the children how much the father in the Bible story loved his son. Talk about ways we can show love in our families.

2. Tell the children to draw each member of their families, including themselves, on a piece of the poster board. If they want to draw their pet on a piece, have them do that, too.

3. Write the sentence "I love my family" on the front of a poster board piece and "God is love" on the back for each child. Then help them write the name under each of the family members they have drawn.

4. Use the hole punch to make a hole in the top of each of the children's poster board pieces. Then tie a piece of yarn through the hole. Give each child a coat hanger and help them tie the other end of the string along the bottom piece of the coat hanger, so that the family member pieces and the piece that says "I love my family" hang like a mobile.

5. Encourage the children to hang their mobiles at home and tell their parents about the Bible story.

Watching for a Son Maze

The son went far away from home and spent all of his money. He needed to get back home to his father. The son wanted to leave the pig pen and go home. The son's father still loved him very much. Use your finger or a pencil to trace the road that the son must take to get home to his father.

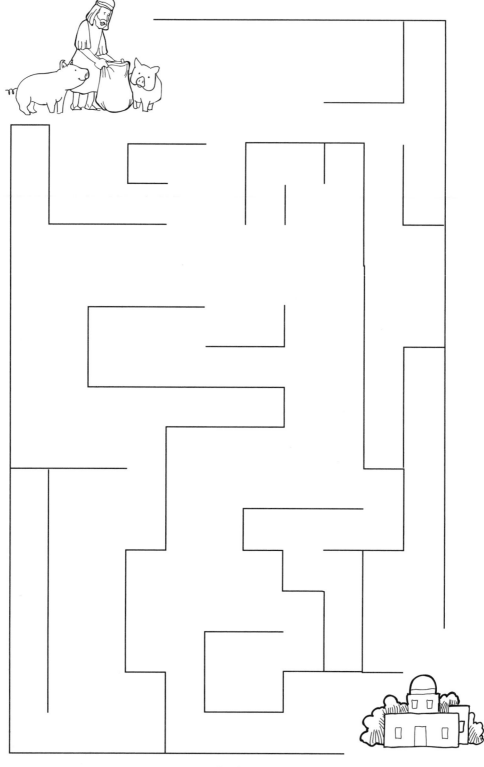

God is love.
1 John 4:16

The solution is on page 96.

The Samaritan • A Good Neighbor

Memory Verse: Love your neighbor as yourself. (Luke 10:27)

The Beaten Man

Luke 10:25-37 (read aloud)

Then tell the Bible story:

One day Jesus told this story to the people. A man was walking along the road to a city called Jericho. The road was out in the desert, so there weren't many people traveling on it. There were robbers hiding along the side of the road. When the man walked by, they jumped out and beat him. The robbers took his money and ran away, leaving the man lying on the ground.

While the man was on the ground, two men passed by. These men worked in the temple. They looked at the man on the ground, but they kept on walking. Finally, a third man came down the road. This man was from Samaria. The hurt man was a Jew. Usually the Jews and the Samaritans did not like each other. But the Samaritan saw that the other man was hurt, so he stopped to help.

The Samaritan put medicine and bandages on the hurt man. Then he put the man on his donkey and took him to an inn where he could rest and get well. The Samaritan gave the innkeeper some money to take care of the hurt man.

Jesus asked the people listening to the story, "Who was a good neighbor to the man who was hurt?" The people answered that the Samaritan man was the good neighbor.

Jesus told this story because He wants us to love each other and to be good neighbors to everyone we meet.

Talk It Over

1. How was the Samaritan man a good neighbor?
2. How can we be good neighbors to each other?

Helping Hands

What You Need

- adhesive bandages
- cotton balls
- gauze
- blanket
- construction paper
- scissors
- markers

What to Do

1. Explain to the children that they will act out a skit about the story of the Good Samaritan. Assign the following parts to the children: man who was hurt, robbers, innkeeper, two men walking to the temple and the Good Samaritan.

2. Read the Bible story aloud and have the children act out their parts as you read. Have the "Good Samaritan" use the bandages, cotton balls, gauze and blanket to care for the man who was hurt.

3. When the children have finished acting out the skit, ask, **What are some ways you can help people who are hurting?** Allow time for the children to answer. Then explain that one way to help people who are hurting or those who are sick is to send them words of encouragement.

4. Give each child a piece of construction paper and have them trace their hands onto the paper. Help them cut out the hand patterns.

5. Give each child a bandage and have them stick it onto the hand pattern. Then help them write encouraging words, such as "Get well soon," "God loves you" or "Hope you feel better" on the hands.

6. Mail the hand prints to someone in the church or community who is sick.

Helping Friends

The Samaritan man stopped to help a man who was hurt. Jesus said that we should try to be like the Samaritan and watch for ways to help others. Look at the bandages below. Color the bandages next to what you will do to help your friends when they are hurting.

Send a card to a friend who is sick.

Say a kind word to a friend who is sad.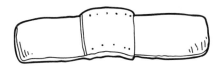

Smile and say hello to all the friends you see today.

Give a hug to a friend who is lonely.

Can you name something else that you can do to help a friend?

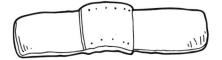

_____

Love your neighbor as yourself.
Luke 10:27

Memory Verse Scrambler

Jesus told the story of the Good Samaritan. The Samaritan man stopped to help a man who was beaten and left beside the road. Jesus told this story so we would understand what it means to be a good neighbor.

Write the words of the Bible verse in the correct order on the lines below.

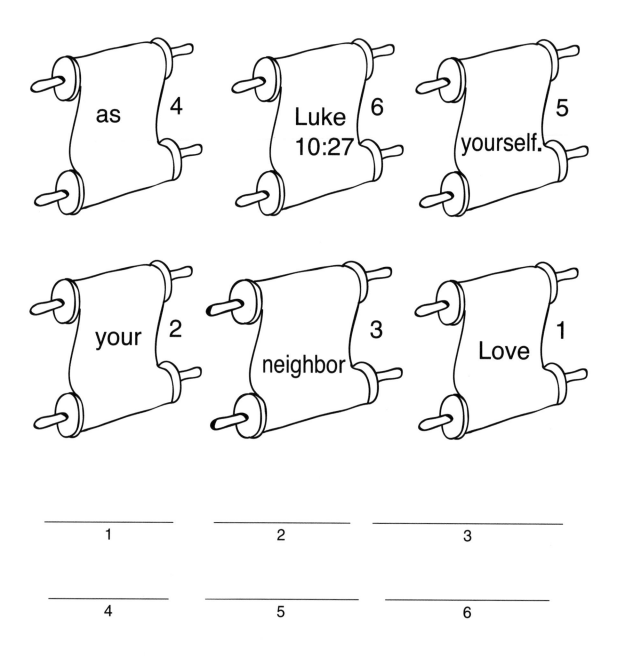

1	2	3

4	5	6

The answers are on page 96.

Hannah • A Mom Who Prayed

Memory Verse: I prayed for this child, and the Lord has granted me what I asked of him.

(1 Samuel 1:27)

The Special Prayer Request

1 Samuel 1:1-20 (read aloud)

Then tell the Bible story:

Hannah and her husband, Elkanah, wanted to have children. But after they had been married a long time they still did not have a baby. Hannah prayed that God would give her a baby. She told God that she was sad and asked Him to give her a child.

Sometimes Hannah was so sad because she did not have a child that she cried. But still she kept on praying to God. Hannah even promised God that if she had a child, she would make sure that the child did God's work.

Suddenly Hannah knew that God had heard her prayer. She was going to have a baby! When her son was born, she named him Samuel. Hannah was so happy to have a son! She and Elkanah praised God for answering their prayers and giving them a son.

Hannah remembered her promise to God. When Samuel grew to be a bigger boy, she took him to be a helper in the temple. Samuel learned to love God, just like his mother, Hannah, did.

Talk It Over

1. What did Hannah ask for in her prayers?
2. How did God answer her prayers?
3. What things can we tell God when we pray?

God Answers Prayers

What You Need

- patterns for the baby below and for Hannah from page 49
- crayons
- scissors
- tape

Before Class

Duplicate Hannah and the baby for each child.

What to Do

1. Give each child a pattern of Hannah and baby Samuel. Have them color the patterns.

2. Help the children cut out the pictures of Hannah and baby Samuel.

3. Go around and cut two small slits in between Hannah's arms as shown with the dashed lines.

4. Show how to put the baby in Hannah's arms where the slits are cut. Put a small piece of tape on the backside to hold baby Samuel in place.

5. Talk about how God answered Hannah's prayers and how He answers our prayers today. Let the children share any prayer requests they may have and then close with prayer.

Do You Pray?

For many years, Hannah prayed that she would have a child. God answered her prayer and Samuel was born. Hannah and her husband praised God for answering the prayer. You can pray, too. Prayer is just talking to God. God loves us and wants us to talk to Him through prayer. Color the pictures of the things below that you pray for. You can pray for all these things, plus more!

FAMILY

FOOD

FRIENDS

TEACHER

A SICK PERSON

I prayed for this child, and the Lord has granted me what I asked of him.
1 Samuel 1:27

Hezekiah • An Obedient King

Memory Verse: We will obey the Lord our God. (Jeremiah 42:6)

Showing the People God's Way

2 Chronicles 30:1-27 (read aloud)

Then tell the Bible story:

Hezekiah was a king who obeyed God. But he did not have an easy job. For many years before Hezekiah was king, the people had done evil things and disobeyed God. Hezekiah knew that he must show the people how important it is to love and obey God.

First, Hezekiah had the temple repaired so that the people would have a place to worship. Then Hezekiah called for all the people to come together to celebrate Passover. The Passover was a special time when the people celebrated the wonderful things that God had done for them in the past. Hezekiah sent messengers throughout the land to call the people together. Some people laughed and made fun of the king's messengers. But other people listened and came to the Passover celebration.

The celebration lasted two weeks. During this time, the people worshipped and praised God. They gave special offerings to God. They played instruments and sang praises to God. The people could not remember when everyone had been so happy. They asked God to forgive them for the ways that they had disobeyed Him in the past. When the Passover celebration was over, the people went back to their homes. When they got home, they threw away the idols (or false gods) that they had been worshipping. From then on, the people wanted to worship the one, true God. Hezekiah had helped the people return to loving God.

talk, talk! Talk It Over

1. What did Hezekiah do to help the people of his country?
2. How can we show that we love God by helping others?

Obeying God Necklace

What You Need

- patterns for Obeying God circles below
- yarn
- round cereal
- markers
- tape
- construction paper
- hole punch

Before Class

Make a copy of the Obeying God circle patterns below for each child. Cut the yarn into 12" lengths (to tie into a necklace). Tightly wrap a piece of tape around one end so that the children can easily string the cereal onto the yarn. Tie a knot in the other end of the string.

What to Do

1. Give each child a copy of the Obeying God circle patterns and have them color in the words and picture.

2. Help the students glue the circles to construction paper and cut them out.

3. Punch a hole in the top of the circles so that they can be strung on the necklace later.

4. Have the children string the cereal on their necklaces. While they are stringing, talk about ways that they can obey God.

5. Show how to string the Obeying God circles onto the middle of the necklace. Have the students continue with stringing cereal until the necklace is complete. Then tie the ends of the yarn together to make the necklace.

How Do You Obey God?

King Hezekiah loved God. He saw that the people had disobeyed God for many years. King Hezekiah knew that this was wrong. First, he fixed the temple because it was in disrepair. Then King Hezekiah planned a special feast for Passover. All the people came together for the feast. The people remembered how much God loved them. Now they would not disobey God anymore. They would obey God and love Him every day.

You can obey God, too, in everything you do. Color the pictures below of what you can do to obey God.

We will obey the Lord our God.
Jeremiah 42:6

Joash • A Caretaker King

Memory Verse: I rejoiced with those who said to me, "Let us go to the house of the Lord." (Psalm 122:1)

A Plan for Rebuilding God's House

2 Chronicles 24:1-14 (read aloud)

Then tell the Bible story:

Joash was a king who loved and obeyed God. He knew the temple must be repaired because the people had no place to worship God until the temple was rebuilt. So Joash told the people that it was time to fix the temple.

But there was one problem. Fixing the temple would cost money. Where would they get the money? King Joash had a plan. He had a special box built and then he put the box outside the gate near the temple. Then King Joash spread the word to all the people that they should bring money to put in the box. The money that was collected in the box would be used to fix up the temple.

The people began to put money in the box. Soon there was plenty of money for fixing the temple! The money was used to buy supplies and pay the people who worked to repair the temple.

When the temple was repaired, there was money left over. The extra money was used to make beautiful decorations for the temple. Once the temple was finished, the people had a place where they could come together to worship God..

talk, talk! Talk It Over

1. What was King Joash's plan for fixing up the temple?
2. What are the things we can do to be helpers in God's house?

Helpers in God's House

What You Need

- pattern for helper's badge below
- several dishpans
- dishwashing liquid
- dish towels/dish cloths
- dusting cloths
- child-size brooms
- poster board
- scissors
- crayons
- glue
- hole punch
- yarn

Before Class

Duplicate the helper's badge below for each child. Cut a 12" length of yarn for each child.

What to Do

1. Explain that just like King Joash helped care for the temple, we can help take care of our church by cleaning the classroom.

2. Set up several stations around the classroom for dusting chairs and tables, sweeping and washing toys. To clean the toys, set up small dish pans with soapy water and have the children wash and dry the toys that can be washed. You might want to dress the children in paint smocks first.

3. Have the children rotate through the different stations so they can do different things to help. While they are working, talk about how we can be helpers in God's house.

4. After they have finished cleaning the room, have the children sit at the table. Give each child a helper's badge pattern and have them color it. When they are finished coloring the badge, show how to glue the badges to poster board and cut them out.

5. Use a hole punch to make a hole in the top of the badge. String yarn through the hole and tie it so the children can wear their badges around their necks.

Your Church Picture

King Joash saw that the temple was in disrepair. The people could not come to worship God until the temple was fixed. So the people brought their money as a special offering. The money was used to fix the temple. The people gave so much that there was money left over! Now people could come to worship God in the temple.

Churches come in all sizes. Draw a picture of your church in the box below.

I rejoiced with those who said to me, "Let us go to the house of the Lord."
Psalm 122:1

Sum 2003

A Coat of Many Colors

Genesis 37:1-3 (read aloud)

Then tell the Bible story:

Joseph was a young man who believed in God. Joseph helped his father and his family by taking care of the flocks of sheep. This was a job that Joseph and all of his brothers did.

When Joseph was 17 years old, his father, Jacob, gave Joseph a special gift. Jacob gave Joseph a beautiful coat. The Bible says that the coat was "richly ornamented." This means that the coat was covered with beautiful decorations. Jacob gave Joseph the coat to show that he loved Joseph very much. Joseph proudly wore the beautiful coat that his father had given him. Later, when he was older, Joseph was a strong leader for God.

Talk It Over

1. What special gift did Jacob give Joseph?
2. Why did Jacob give Joseph such a special gift?
3. How do your parents show that they love you?
4. How can you show your parents that you love them?

Joseph's Coat

What You Need

• Joseph's coat pattern from page 59
• scraps of fabric, felt, ribbon or braid
• glue
• scissors
• construction paper

Before Class

Duplicate Joseph's coat pattern from page 59 for each child. Cut the fabric, felt, ribbon and braid into small pieces.

What to Do

1. Explain to the children that the Bible says that Joseph's coat was beautifully decorated, and that they will be decorating a coat to remind them of Joseph's coat.

2. Give each child a coat pattern and a piece of construction paper. Help them cut out and glue the coat pattern onto the construction paper.

3. Provide the small pieces of fabric, felt, ribbon or braid and have the children glue these pieces on their coat pattern to make a "beautifully decorated" coat like Joseph's.

4. Set aside the coats to allow the glue to dry. Remind the children that Joseph's father gave Joseph the coat because he loved Joseph very much. Explain that we can show our love for our parents when we obey them.

Joseph's Connect the Dots

Joseph's father loved him very much. His father gave him a coat as a special gift. The coat was made of pretty cloth and it was very beautiful. Joseph loved the gift that his father gave him.

Start with the letter A and draw a line from letter to letter through the alphabet to make Joseph's coat. Then color it with many colors.

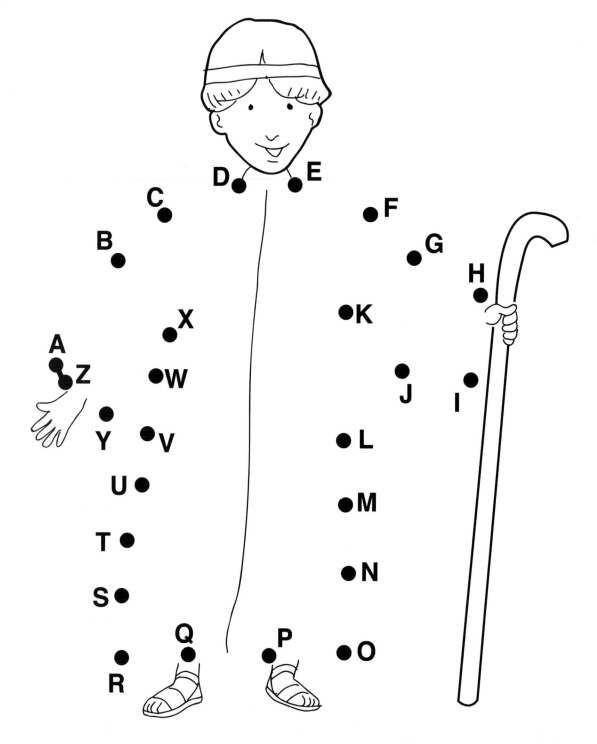

Children, obey your parents in the Lord, for this is right.
Ephesians 6:1

 **Lydia** • **The Christian Saleswoman**

Memory Verse: I am not ashamed of the gospel. (Romans 1:16)

A Woman Who Sold Purple Cloth

 Acts 16:11-15 (read aloud)

Then tell the Bible story:

Paul was a missionary who traveled to different towns and cities telling people about Jesus. One day Paul came to the city of Philippi. While they were staying in the city, Paul and the other missionaries who traveled with him went outside the city gate. They walked down to the river because they wanted a quiet place where they could pray.

But Paul found other people at the river. A group of women was there. Lydia was talking to the group. Lydia had a job selling purple cloth. She and the other women had heard of God. But Paul was able to tell them about Jesus and how much Jesus loves everyone.

Lydia opened her heart and became a follower of Jesus. The other members of Lydia's family believed in Jesus then, too. Lydia and her whole family were baptized. Then they invited Paul and the other missionaries to come to their home to visit.

 talk, talk!

Talk It Over

1. Remind the children that a missionary is a person who travels to other places to tell people about Jesus. Ask, What did Paul and his missionary friends find when they went down to the river to pray?

2. Who was Lydia? What did Paul tell Lydia and the other women?

3. How can we tell our friends about Jesus?

Lydia's Pouch

What You Need

- purple felt, 9" x 12"
- buttons, rick-rack, ribbon or braid
- glue
- scissors
- stapler (optional)
- tape (optional)

What to Do

1. Remind the children that Lydia sold purple cloth to people who would then make clothing or other things with it. Explain that they will be making a pouch from purple cloth.

2. Give each child a piece of purple felt. Have the children fold the felt in half and then help them glue the sides together to make a pouch. You may want to reinforce the glue by placing a couple of staples along each side of the pouch. Cover the staples with clear tape to avoid injury.

3. Have the children decorate their pouches by gluing on buttons, braid or ribbons. Allow the glue to dry. Explain that the children can use their pouches to carry small items, such as pencils, paper or their offering money.

Where Can You Learn?

Paul told Lydia and her friends the good news about Jesus. It's good to learn about Jesus so that you can tell your friends about Him, too. Where can you learn about Jesus? Point to the pictures below that show good ways to learn about Jesus. Color your favorite way to learn about Jesus.

FRIENDS

FAMILY

BIBLE

CHURCH

I am not ashamed of the gospel.
Romans 1:16

 • A Gift-giver

Memory Verse: Do everything in love. (1 Corinthians 16:14)

Showing Her Love for Jesus

Mark 14:1-9 (read aloud)

Then tell the Bible story:

One day Jesus and His disciples visited a man named Simon. While they were sitting in Simon's home, a woman named Mary came to visit, too. Mary and her family were Jesus' friends. Mary brought a gift for Jesus — a bottle of very expensive perfume.

Mary broke open the jar of perfume. Then she poured the perfume on Jesus' hair. She did this to show how much she loved Jesus. The wonderful smell of the perfume must have filled the whole room!

Some of the people who were watching began to talk about Mary. They thought that she should have sold the bottle of expensive perfume and used the money to help other people. They thought that Mary had wasted the perfume by pouring it on Jesus' head.

But Jesus did not think that Mary had wasted the perfume. Jesus told the people to stop talking about Mary. Jesus knew that Mary was showing how much she loved Him. Jesus praised Mary for showing her love with the gift of the perfume.

Talk It Over

1. What gift did Mary bring to Jesus?
2. How did Mary show she loved Jesus?
3. How can we show Jesus that we love Him?

Loving Hands Place Mat

What You Need

- several small, scented candles
- art smocks (men's old shirts)
- tempera paint
- plate
- paper
- disposable hand wipes
- markers
- clear, self-stick plastic
- scissors

Do everything in love.
1 Corinthians 16:14

What to Do

1. Remind the children that Mary showed her love for Jesus by pouring perfume on Jesus' hair.

2. Have the children pass around the scented candles, smelling each one. Say, **Mary's gift of love had a very sweet smell, like these candles have a sweet smell. The other people in the room didn't just see her gift — they could smell the sweet fragrance, too.** Ask the children how they can use what they have to show love to Jesus. *nice to people, love family, help put toys away*

3. Give each child a piece of paper. Pour paint onto a plate. Have each child place his or her whole hand, with the palm down, into the paint. Then have the child press his or her palm onto the paper. Do this for both hands. Be sure to wipe the children's hands clean before allowing them to leave the paint area.

4. When the paint is dry, write the memory verse (Do everything in love. 1 Corinthians 16:14) across the bottom of each paper. Then cover both sides of the paper with clear, self-stick plastic. Explain that they can take their hand prints home and use them as a place mat.

5. Lead the children in saying the Bible verse together. Talk about ways we can show that we love each other and that we love Jesus.

Words That Show Love

Mary loved Jesus very much. She showed her love by giving Him a gift of perfume. She put the perfume on Jesus' head to show her love for Him.

We can show love by the way we talk to each other. Look at what these children are saying. Circle the pictures that show love.

Do everything in love.
1 Corinthians 16:14

Melchizedek • A Thankful King

Memory Verse: This Melchizedek was king of Salem and priest of God Most High. (Hebrews 7:1)

A Leader for God

Genesis 14:17-20, Hebrews 7:1-4 (read aloud)

Then tell the Bible story:

Long before Jesus was born, there was a man whose name was Melchizedek. The Bible says that Melchizedek's name means "king of peace." Melchizedek was the king of Salem and a priest who worshipped God.

One day, Abraham, a great man who served God, was coming home from a battle. Abraham and his soldiers had won the battle. Abraham met Melchizedek along the road. Melchizedek reminded Abraham that he had won the battle because of God's help. Melchizedek thanked God for helping Abraham win the battle. Because he was thankful, too, Abraham gave Melchizedek an offering for God.

Melchizedek served God with his whole heart and helped others around him serve God, too.

 ## Talk It Over

1. What was the meaning of Melchizedek's name?
2. Melchizedek was thankful to God — for what things can we thank God?

Color Nature Walk

What You Need

- small paper bags
- construction paper
- glue

Before Class

You will need a different color of construction paper cut into a 4" x 4" square for each pair of students. Be sure the colors are nature colors, such as brown, orange, green and so on.

What to Do

1. Remind the children that Melchizedek remembered to praise God. Point out that one way to say "thanks" to God is by talking about all of the beauty in nature. Explain that the class will take a nature walk to see some of the beautiful things God has made for our world.

2. Arrange the children in pairs and give each pair a paper bag and one square of construction paper. Have them glue this square on the outside of their bag and explain that they will be looking for nature items of that color.

3. Remind the children that there are some things they can bring back in their bags, such as leaves, nuts, pine cones and so on that they find on the ground. Explain that they will see some things, such as flowers, trees and so on that they can look at and enjoy, but they cannot bring them back.

4. Lead the group in the nature walk. While you walk, talk about how many different colors we see in nature. Encourage the children to always think of God and say "thank You" when they see the beauty of nature.

5. Return to the classroom and allow time for each pair to "show and tell" the items that they collected.

I Am Thankful

Melchizedek was a priest. His name means "king of peace." The Bible says that Melchizedek was thankful for many things.

Draw something below for which you are thankful.

This Melchizedek was king of Salem and priest of God Most High.
Hebrews 7:1

Micah • A Preacher of Promises

Memory Verse: *Not one of all the Lord's good promises...failed. (Joshua 21:45)*

Seeing God's Promises

Micah 5:2-4 (read aloud)

Then tell the Bible story:

Micah lived many, many years before Jesus was born. God gave Micah the job of preaching to the people. Micah warned the people that they must stop doing bad things. Micah also told the people that they needed to love God with all their hearts.

During the time that Micah was preaching, God made a special promise to Micah. God promised Micah that a Savior would be born. This Savior would be born in the town of Bethlehem. The Savior that God promised would be Jesus!

God kept His promises to Micah, didn't He? Many, many years later, Jesus was born in a town called Bethlehem. He came to be our Savior, just like God told Micah He would.

Talk It Over

1. What was Micah's job?
2. What promise did God make to Micah?
3. How did God keep His promise?

Promise Reminders

 ## What You Need

- baking soda
- corn starch
- cold water
- cooktop
- water-based acrylic paints
- art smocks (men's old shirts)
- paint brushes
- black marker

Before Class

You can mix the dough recipe before class or, if time allows, have the children help you mix it. Depending on the size of your group, you may need to make more than one batch.

What to Do

1. Mix 2 cups of baking soda, 1 cup of corn starch, and 1¼ cups of cold water in a sauce pan. Bring it to a boil and let it boil for one minute, stirring until it has the consistency of mashed potatoes.

2. Pour the dough into a bowl. Cover and let it cool completely.

3. Knead the dough until it is smooth. Store in an airtight container in the refrigerator.

4. When you are ready to use the dough, remove it from the refrigerator and let it come to room temperature.

5. Give each child a dough portion that is a little smaller than a baseball. Show them how to press the dough out flat.

6. Have the children roll out "snakes" with their dough and then press the rolls together to form the shape of a rainbow. Explain that the rainbow is one reminder of the way that God keeps His promises.

7. Allow the dough to dry completely. Then have the children paint their rainbows.

8. When the paint has dried, write the words "God keeps His promises" somewhere on the rainbow, using a black marker. Tell the children that this rainbow can be their reminder that God keeps His promises to us, just like the promise He gave to Micah.

Rainbow Treats

What You Need

- small paper cups
- aluminum foil
- thin craft sticks
- several juice flavors
- freezer

What to Do

1. Remind the children that the Bible is full of promises from God, just like the one He made to Micah. Explain that the rainbow was a sign of God's promise to Noah that floods would never again cover the whole earth. Explain that the class will be making Rainbow Treats as a reminder of that promise. (Depending on your class time, you might want to extend this activity over a few sessions or make the treats before class.)

2. Give each child a small paper cup and help them write their names or initials on the outside of the cup.

3. Have them help you pour a small amount of juice (about ¼" to ½" deep) into each cup. Place the cups in the freezer until the juice is hard frozen.

4. Pull the cups out of the freezer and have the students help you pour another layer of juice (a different color) into each cup.

5. Cover each cup with a piece of aluminum foil, then have the students help you put a craft stick through the center of the foil and push it down in the cup until it touches the frozen juice layer. Place the cups back in the freezer. The foil will hold the craft stick in place until the second layer of juice freezes to hold it.

6. Continue adding juice and freezing it until you have as many layers as desired. When all the layers are hard frozen, help the children peel off the paper cups. Point out the colors of the Rainbow Treats and let the children enjoy eating them.

The Musicians • Praising God

Memory Verse: I will make music to the Lord. (Judges 5:3)

Praising God with Music

1 Chronicles 25:1-8 (read aloud)

Then tell the Bible story:

During the time that David was king, God's house (called the temple) was a very busy place in the city of Jerusalem. Many people came to the temple to worship God. King David saw that there were lots of jobs to be done in the temple. So David found people who wanted to work in the temple. He gave them jobs to do so they could serve God.

David chose 228 people to work in the temple as musicians. The musicians led the people in thanking and praising God. They sang and played harps, lyres and cymbals.

Anyone who had learned how to sing or play an instrument could ask to have a job as a musician. So both young people and older people were chosen to be musicians. These people then came to work at the temple and praise God with their music. The temple was a joyful place, filled with music.

Talk It Over

1. What job did the musicians do in the temple?
2. What songs do you know that praise God?

Joyful Jingles

What You Need

- chenille wire
- craft foam
- small jingle bells
- scissors
- markers
- hole punch

Before Class

Trace a quarter on craft foam and cut out the circle. Punch a hole at the top of the circle. You will need three or four foam circles for each child.

What to Do

1. Remind the children how the temple musicians praised God through music. Explain that the class will make Joyful Jingles to play while you sing.

2. Give each child a chenille wire and three or four foam circles.

3. Draw several musical notes on the board for the children to look at as examples, then have the children draw a musical note on each of their foam circles.

4. Have the children string some jingle bells and foam circles on the chenille wire.

5. Help them bring the two ends of the chenille wire together and twist so that the wire stays in the shape of a circle.

6. Encourage the children to wear the Joyful Jingle on their wrist or hold it in their hands. Lead the children in singing some familiar praise songs while they play their Joyful Jingles.

Name the Instrument

The musicians had special jobs in the temple. They led people in praising God with music. The musicians sang songs and played instruments. The temple was filled with the sound of music praising God. How does your church use music to praise God? Color each instrument below as you say its name.

I will make music to the Lord.
Judges 5:3

When Do You Sing?

The musicians sang and played their instruments to praise God. Their songs filled the temple with praise. Do you like to sing or play instruments? Do you sing songs about God only at special times? Or is any time a good time to sing about God? Circle the pictures below that show when you sing. Then color all of the pictures.

Should you sing when you are happy?

Should you sing when you are sad?

Should you sing when you feel lonely?

Should you sing when you are alone?

Should you sing when you are with friends?

I will make music to the Lord.
Judges 5:3

The Sick Woman • Healed by Faith

Memory Verse: [Jesus] said to her, "Daughter, your faith has healed you." (Mark 5:34)

Just a Touch

Mark 5:24-34 (read aloud)

Then tell the Bible story:

A large crowd of people was following Jesus and His disciples. There were so many people that sometimes they bumped into each other. One of the people in the crowd was a woman who had been sick for many years. This woman had been to many doctors. She spent all of her money trying to find something that would make her well. But nothing seemed to help her. So she came to Jesus because she knew that He had performed miracles and made sick people well.

As Jesus moved through the crowd of people, the woman decided that maybe if she could just touch Jesus' robe it would make her well. So as He passed by she reached out and touched just the edge of His robe. As soon as she touched His robe, she knew something good had happened. The woman was well!

Jesus knew that something had happened, too. He asked the people standing close to Him, "Who touched My clothes?" Jesus' disciples were surprised that He asked this question. They told Jesus that with all the people crowded around there were many who had touched Him.

But Jesus knew that a miracle had happened. He kept looking to find the person who had touched His robe. The woman knelt down at Jesus' feet. She was afraid of what Jesus might say or do. But Jesus was not angry with the woman. Jesus just wanted to tell the woman that she was healed because she showed such great faith. The woman had faith to believe that simply by touching Jesus' robe she could be well.

talk, talk! Talk It Over

1. Why did the woman come to see Jesus?
2. What did the woman think could make her well?
3. How can we show that we have faith in Jesus?

Clothesline Story

What You Need

- white construction paper
- crayons
- yarns or rope
- clothespins

Before Class

Cut the construction paper in half so that each child has a half-piece.

What to Do

1. Give each child a piece of white construction paper.

2. Assign one of the following parts of the Bible story to each child:

    1. large group of people following Jesus

    2. woman touches Jesus' robe

    3. the disciples tell Jesus they don't know who touched His robe

    4. woman knelt at Jesus' feet

    5. woman was healed by Jesus because of her faith

If the class is large, you may want to make two story clotheslines.

3. Have the children draw their assigned part of the story on the construction paper.

4. Attach the yarn or rope to the backs of two chairs and position the chairs so that the clothesline is pulled tight.

5. Have each child show his or her picture to the group and tell what happened. Then let them attach their pictures to the clothesline with a clothespin. Help the children hang their story pictures on the clothesline in the order their scenes happened in the story.

Places We Go

Think about the places you go each day. Jesus cares about you and watches over you, wherever you go. Put a √ by the places you will go this week, then color the pictures.

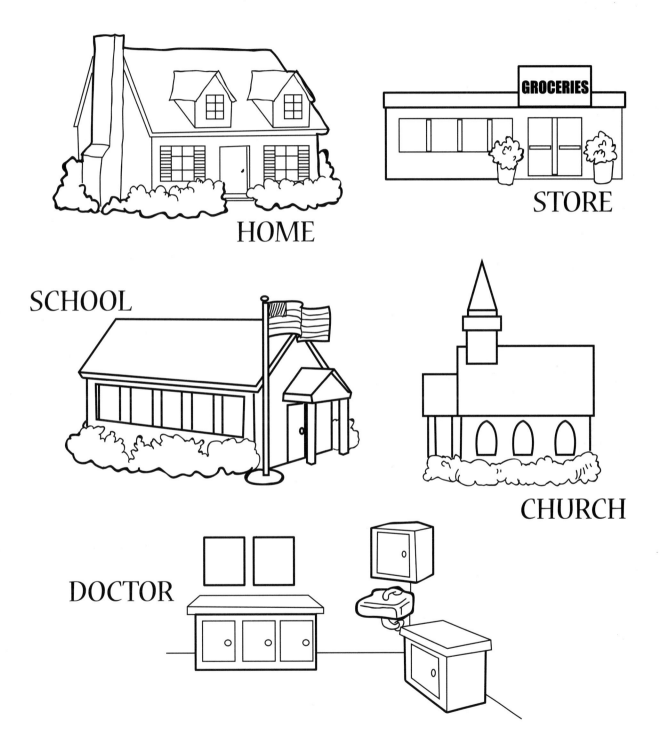

HOME

STORE

SCHOOL

CHURCH

DOCTOR

[Jesus] said to her, "Daughter, your faith has healed you."
Mark 5:34

Simon of Cyrene • A Helper

Memory Verse: For God so loved the world that he gave his one and only Son, that whoever believes in him shall not perish but have eternal life. (John 3:16)

Carrying the Cross for Jesus

Matthew 27:27-35 (read aloud)

Then tell the Bible story:

Jesus was preaching and teaching. People listened to Him. But some of the people did not want Jesus to say that He was God's Son. These people wanted to kill Jesus. Jesus knew that the people wanted to kill Him, but He did not run away. The soldiers who captured Him beat Him with a whip. They spit on Jesus and hit Him with a stick. Then these soldiers led Jesus through the streets of the city on His way to be killed.

In the crowded city streets, the soldiers made Jesus carry His own cross. Jesus was weak because of how He had been beaten. He wasn't strong enough to carry the cross. So the soldiers pointed to a man in the crowd. The man's name was Simon and he was from the city of Cyrene. The soldiers made Simon pick up the cross and carry it the rest of the way to the place where they planned to kill Jesus. The Bible does not tell us any more about Simon. We only know that Simon helped Jesus on that terrible day when He was crucified.

The good news is that when Jesus died on the cross, He showed how much He loved us. Because Jesus died on the cross, we can come to know God.

Talk It Over

1. Why did some of the people want to kill Jesus?
2. How did Simon of Cyrene help Jesus?
3. How did Jesus show that He loves us?

Jesus Loves Me Mirrors

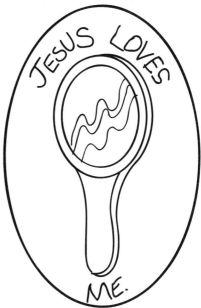

What You Need

- small, pocket-sized mirrors
- glue
- poster board
- markers
- scissors

What to Do

1. Remind the children that Jesus died on the cross because He loves each one of us. Explain that the class will be making mirror posters to remind us that Jesus loves us.

2. Give each child a mirror. Tell the children to look in the mirror to see someone Jesus loves.

3. Help the children cut out a piece of poster board that is the same shape as the mirror, but 1-2" wider so there is room to write on the poster board.

4. Help the children glue the mirror onto the poster board. Allow the glue to dry.

5. Help the children write "Jesus Loves" on the poster board above the mirror and "Me" on the poster board underneath the mirror. Suggest that the children keep the mirror poster in their bedroom as a reminder each day that Jesus loves them.

Helpers

The soldiers hurt Jesus, then they wanted Him to carry the heavy wooden cross through the streets of the city. Jesus was too weak to carry the cross. So the soldiers picked Simon of Cyrene out of the crowd of people standing on the street. Simon helped Jesus by carrying the cross for Him. We can be helpers, too. As you color the pictures below, talk about how they show helping.

For God so loved the world that he gave his one and only Son, that whoever believes in him shall not perish but have eternal life.
John 3:16

Titus • A Church Helper

Memory Verse: *In everything set them an example by doing what is good.* (Titus 2:7)

Lessons in a Letter

Titus 3:1-15 (read aloud)

Then tell the Bible story:

Titus lived on an island called Crete, where he worked in the church. Titus knew Paul, a famous preacher who traveled from town to town.

Paul wrote a letter to Titus. The letter told Titus how to help the people in Crete be the kind of people God wanted them to be. The letter told everyone in the church — older men, older women, younger men and younger women — how they should live.

Titus told the people all the things that Paul said in the letter. Titus helped the people see that they should love each other and love God, too.

Today, there is a book in our Bible called Titus. It is the letter that Paul wrote to Titus a long time ago. It reminds us that we should love God and love each other.

Talk It Over

1. Have you ever received a letter?
2. What was important about the letter Titus received?

Helpers Banner

I can be a helper, too.

What You Need

- newsprint or poster paper (4'-6' long)
- washable tempera paint
- disposable pie plate
- old newspapers
- paint smocks
- disposable hand wipes

Before Class

Write "I can be a helper, too" in large letters on the newsprint or poster paper.

What to Do

1. Remind the children that Titus was a helper to the church people in Crete and a helper to Paul, too. Ask the children to name ways that they can help each other.

2. Spread old newspapers on the floor to catch the extra paint. Put the newsprint or poster paper on top of the newspaper. Call the students' attention to the sentence "I can be a helper, too."

3. Help the children into paint smocks (men's old shirts work well).

4. Pour some tempera paint in the pie plate.

5. Help the students carefully dip both of their hands into the paint. Then have them make hand prints on the paper. Guide the children in placing their hand prints so that they circle around the "I can be a helper, too" sentence.

6. Be sure to thoroughly wipe the paint from the children's hands.

7. After the hand prints are dry, display the banner in the classroom. Remind the children of the different ways that they can be helpers in the classroom.

Showing Love

Titus was a helper to the church people in Crete. He told the people that they should always be kind and show love to each other. We can show love in our families by being kind, too. Look at the picture below. As you color each picture, talk about how these people are showing love and kindness in their families.

In everything set them an example by doing what is good.
Titus 2:7

The Wise Builder • Trusting in the Rock

Memory Verse: Everyone who hears these words of mine and puts them into practice is like a wise man who built his house on the rock. (Matthew 7:24)

A House on Solid Ground

Matthew 7:24-29 (read aloud)

Then tell the Bible story:

One day Jesus told this story to the people. There were two men who were building houses. Jesus said that one of the men was wise and the other man was foolish. The foolish man built his house on sandy ground. This ground was soft, like ground that is near a river or stream. The wise man built his house on a rock — ground that was hard and solid. Both of the houses looked nice, until it started to rain.

When the storm came, the water in the stream rose up like a flood. It was very windy and the wind beat against the sides of the houses. The wise man, who had built his house on the solid rock, did not have to worry. His house was not hurt by the storm. The man was safe and dry until the storm stopped. But the foolish man who had built his house on the sand had big problems. The wind, rain and flood made his house fall down. The foolish man's house fell down with a big crash.

Jesus told the people that the foolish man is like a person who does not follow God. When the hard times come along, someone who doesn't follow God can end up with a big mess — just like the house that crashed. Jesus said that the wise man was like a person who makes God a part of his life. When hard times come along, then that person can know that God will take care of him. We can be like the wise man who built on the rock. We can trust God and He will take care of us.

Talk It Over

1. Where did the foolish man build his house?
2. Where did the wise man build his house?
3. How can we be like the wise man?

Wise Rocks and Shifting Sand

What You Need

- medium-size rocks
- sink or pan of water
- paper towels
- paint
- empty baby food jars
- colored sand (several colors)
- foil pie plates
- plastic spoons
- Christian stickers

What to Do

1. Remind the children that the two men in the Bible story chose different ways to build their houses. Explain that the class will be working with both rock and sand to see how different they are.

2. Give each child a medium-size rock. Have them wash it in the sink or pan of water and then dry it thoroughly using a paper towel. Explain that this is their "wise rock."

3. Suggest some words the students could paint on their wise rock such as "Trust God," "God loves me," "God's Word is our rock," etc. Then help the children paint the words on their rock.

4. Set the rocks aside to dry.

5. Let the children look at sand and see how different it is from the rock. Give them a small bit of sand to hold in their hands and talk about ways that the sand is different from the rock they just painted.

6. Divide the colored sand into pie plates. Give each child a baby food jar. Show how to put spoonfuls of sand into the jar in thin layers, alternating different colors of sand. Remind them to keep the jars on the table — if they shake them, then the colored layers will mix.

7 Have the children continue with different colors of sand until they have filled their jars to the tops. Instruct them to leave enough room in the top for you to tightly close the jar lid.

8. Give each child a sticker to put on top of the jar.

9. Remind the children that God wants us to build our lives on Him — like the man who built his house on the rock.

Like a Wise Man

Jesus told a story about two men who built houses. One man built his house on ground that was hard like a rock. The other man built his house on soft, sandy ground. Then Jesus said that a storm came. When the wind blew and the rain fell, the house built on hard ground was safe. But the house that was built on sand crashed in because of the storm. Jesus said the man who built his house on rock was a wise man. The man was wise because he loved and obeyed God. Jesus wants us to be "wise men," too. How can we be like the wise man who built his house on the rock? Circle the things below that will help you be like the wise man.

*Everyone who hears these words of mine and puts them into practice
is like a wise man who built his house on the rock.*
Matthew 7:24

Wise Man Picture

Jesus told a story of two men who were building houses. The wise man built his house on hard ground. When the rain and storms came, his house was safe. The foolish man built his house on sandy ground. When the storms came, his house fell down. Jesus said that when we love and obey Him, we are like the wise man because we are building our lives on solid ground. Draw a picture in the box below of the wise man and the foolish man, building their houses.

Everyone who hears these words of mine and puts them into practice
is like a wise man who built his house on the rock.
Matthew 7:24

Memory Verse: "I tell you the truth," [Jesus] said, "this poor widow has put in more than all the others." (Luke 21:3)

Two Faithful Coins

Luke 21:1-4 (read aloud)

Then tell the Bible story:

One day Jesus was at the temple, where the people came to worship. He watched as people came into the temple. There were large boxes near the doors of the temple. The people who came to the temple dropped their offering money into the boxes.

While Jesus was watching, He saw many rich people walk up and drop their money into the boxes. Then He saw a poor woman walk up to the offering box. This woman's husband was dead and she did not have very much money. When she got to the offering box, she dropped two coins into it. The two coins were not worth very much. They were probably a lot like the pennies we have today.

Right away, Jesus told the people who were standing near Him to look at the woman. Jesus said that she had given the best gift of all, even though it was just two small coins. The rich people had given nice offering gifts, but they still had a lot of money left to spend on themselves. When the poor woman gave the two coins, she was giving all that she had.

Talk It Over

1. What offering gift did the woman give at the temple?
2. What did Jesus think about the woman's gift?

Tic-Tac-Toe Toss

What You Need

- small bean bag
- brightly-colored poster board
- markers
- X and O patterns from below

Before Class

Make five copies of the X and O patterns below. Cut out the X's and O's. Use a marker to draw a large tic-tac-toe grid on the poster board.

What to Do

1. Arrange the children into nine small groups and assign each group one of the following words or phrases: widow, Luke 21:1-4, temple, boxes for offering, Jesus, offering, Bible, rich people and coins. If your group is small, you can assign a word to each child or even several words to a child.

2. Remind the children of the Bible story you just read about the woman and her offering. Have each group write their word or phrase in large letters in one space on the tic-tac-toe grid. Then have each group draw a picture on the grid to illustrate what their word means. For the Bible reference, suggest that they may want to draw a Bible that is opened to the book of Luke.

3. After they have finished all the squares on the grid, place the tic-tac-toe board on the floor. Have the children stand around the board in a circle. Divide the children into two teams and give one team the "Os" and the other team the "Xs."

4. Have the children take turns tossing the bean bag onto the board. When they land on a square, have them tell what is on the square and how it is a part of the Bible story. Then have them place their X or O on that square. The first team to get three X's or O's in a row wins the game.

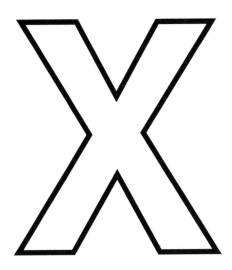
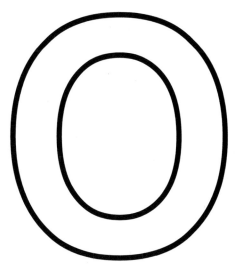

The Woman with an Offering

Read the story by using the pictures.

One day Jesus was at the temple. Jesus saw people put their

in the offering box. Then a  walked into the temple. She put

her offering in the box. It was just  . Some people

put lots of  in the box. When Jesus saw what the

 gave, He told the people to look at her. Jesus said that

the  had given the best  of all. That's

because the  gave all that she had.

"I tell you the truth," [Jesus] said, "this poor widow has put in more than all the others."
Luke 21:3

Zerubbabel • Church Leader

Memory Verse: And all the people gave a great shout of praise to the Lord. (Ezra 3:11)

Rebuilding the Temple

Ezra 3:1-11 (read aloud)

Then tell the Bible story:

The people of Israel were kept as prisoners in another country for many years. Finally, it was time for them to go back to their homes.

When the people got back to their own country, they were sad to see that their temple had been torn down. Zerubbabel led the people in rebuilding the temple. He asked all the people to help, and they did. The people looked to God for instructions and help in rebuilding the temple correctly. The people gave their time and money so that the work could begin. They knew they would soon be able to worship God in the temple again.

When they finished the work, the people and Zerubbabel were so happy! They did not forget to thank God for leading them as they fixed the temple.

Talk It Over

1. What was the job that needed to be done?
2. What did Zerubbabel do?
3. How can you be a helper in your church?

93

Helping Hands Flower Pot

What You Need

- construction paper
- scissors
- glue or tape
- pattern for flower pot, page 95
- craft sticks

Before Class

Duplicate the flower pot pattern on page 95 for each child.

What to Do

1. Remind the children that Zerubbabel helped to fix the temple and that we can be helpers, too.

2. Give each child several pieces of construction paper. Have them place their hands on the paper with their fingers slightly spread apart. Trace around their hands. Repeat this several times on different colors of paper.

3. Have the children cut out the hands and then have them write on the hands different ways that they can be a helper (examples: "help my parents with chores," "be kind to my younger brother/sister," "help pick up the classroom," "share with my friends" and so on).

4. Help the children glue or tape a craft stick on the back of each hand print. They should position the stick on the lower part of the hand print so that some of the stick extends off the hand print like a flower stem.

5. Give each child a copy of the flower pot and have them color and cut it out.

6. Go around and make a cut on the dashed line in the middle of the pot. Help the children insert their completed hand print flowers into the pot, so they look like flowers growing in a pot.

7. Turn the flower pot over and help the children glue or tape the ends of the sticks to the paper to secure them in place.

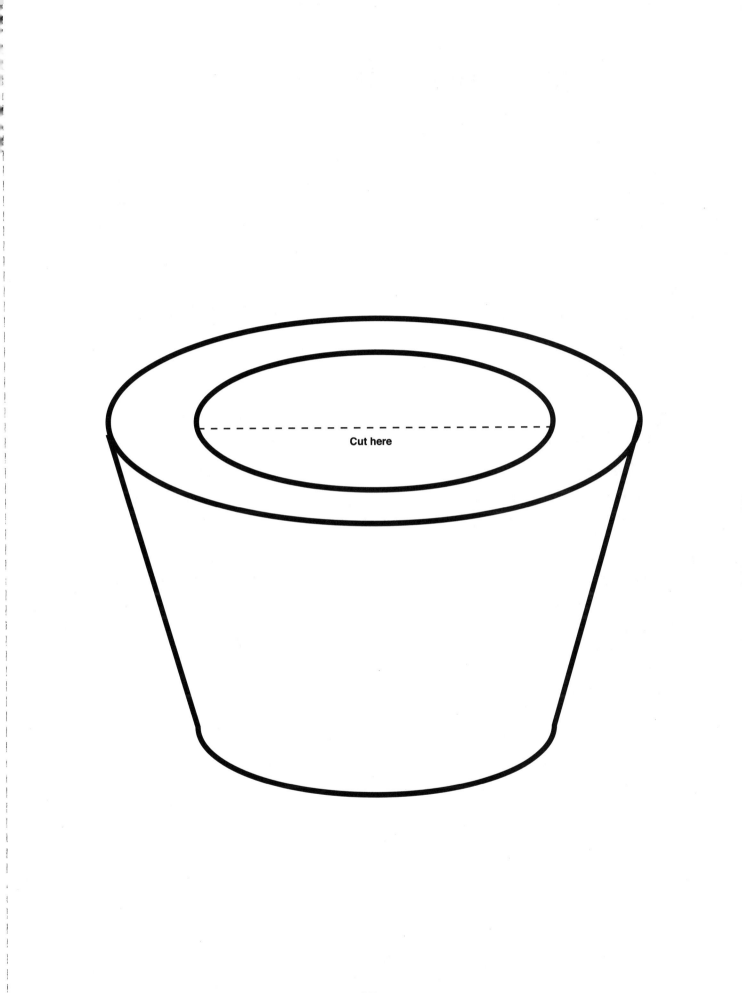

Cut here

Answers

Barnabas
Barnabas Fill-In, page 15
Do not <u>forget</u> to do <u>good</u> and to <u>share</u> with <u>others</u>. (Hebrews 13:16)

The Boy & a Lunch
Sharing Maze, page 24

Centurion
Centurion Fill-In, page 28
faith

Centurion Word Balloons, page 29
Stand firm in the faith. 1 Corinthians 16:13

Deborah
Deborah's Memory Verse Code, page 32
If any of <u>you</u> lacks <u>wisdom</u>, he should ask <u>God</u>…and it will be <u>given</u> to <u>him</u>. James 1:5

Elisha
Elisha Memory Verse Scramble, page 35
We too will serve the Lord. Joshua 24:18

Epaphras
The Path to Rome, page 38

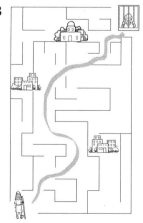

The Loving Father
Watching for a Son Maze, page 42

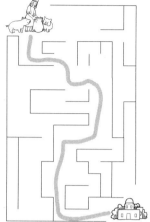

The Samaritan
Memory Verse Scrambler, page 46
Love your neighbor as yourself. Luke 10:27

Joseph
Joseph's Connect the Dots, page 60

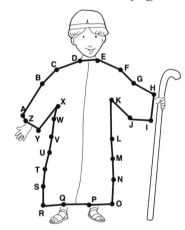

A Woman & Offering
The Woman with an Offering, page 92
One day Jesus was at the temple. Jesus saw people put their <u>coins</u> in the offering box. Then a <u>woman</u> walked into the temple. She put her offering in the box. It was just <u>two coins</u>. Some people put lots of <u>coins</u> in the box. When Jesus saw what the <u>woman</u> gave, He told the people to look at her. Jesus said that the <u>woman</u> had given the best <u>gift</u> of all. That's because the <u>woman</u> gave all that she had.